THE BRADFORD FIRE

1920

How A Big Fire Changed A Small Town

Bradford Church of the Brethren
Historical Committee

Scott D. Trostel

Bradford Church of the Brethren
120 W. Oakwwod St.
Bradford, Ohio 45308

Printed in the United States of America

by Cam-Tech Publishing

First Edition

23456789

Layout and production services provided by:
CAM-TECH PUBLISHING
P.O. BOX 341
FLETCHER, OHIO 45326-0341

ISBN No. 0-925436-13-5

ACKNOWLEDGEMENTS

The idea for this book came about through Vaughn Kniesly and the other members of our Bradford Church of the Brethren Historical Committee. It has ended up being a fund raiser for our church's Building Fund.

We especially want to thank the ones who were willing to be interviewed, and we remember them for the valuable information they shared with us, and for the incidents they remembered. The ones interviewed principally were Bill Elson, Harvey Medlam, Opal Patty, Sarah Harrison, Lillian Baughman, Adelaide Wilson, and Amos Carine. Although not all of these had long stories to tell, we are glad for their input, regardless how great or small.

We highly esteem Scott Trostel. Without him it is doubtful whether or not this book would ever have been published.

We also want to note, many of the photos marked ''Bradford Public Library'' are from the Bill Shannon collection.

We want to thank Irene Ganger for sharing her artistic ability by creating the artwork on the front cover. She painted the nighttime fire scene from a daytime photo of the remains of one of the buildings which actually burned in the Bradford fire. Since no known photographs exist of the actual fire, Irene's painting is as close as we can come to visualizing what that awesome night looked like.

We also thank everyone else who so graciously and thoughtfully contributed in many other ways, and encouraged us in this project.

The Brethren Historical Committee:

Earl Landis, Chairman	Mary Stover
Ruth Royer, Secretary	Vaughn Kniesly
Janice Hocker, Church Historian	
Pastor Sandford Christophel, Ex-officio	

DEDICATION

We dedicate this book to the many citizens of Bradford who through the years have loved their community, who have had a resilient determination in the face of many difficulties, and who have had a strong faith and trust in God to guide them onward.

INTRODUCTION

Since our Committee first talked about publishing this book in September of 1992, the number of folks in the Bradford area who could personally remember this fire has dwindled to just a few. Several of those interviewed for this book have since passed on to their reward, including Bill Elson and Opal Patty. We realize now that we have done this project none too soon! In fact, if we would have started even a year later, some of the contents of this book would have died with the individuals.

As is true in our daily lives, what begins as a common ordinary day often turns out to be the most significant day of all. Often the defining events and turning points happen when we least expect. This is exactly what happened in this small railroad town of Bradford, Ohio, in early August 1920. Suddenly, literally overnight, the whole scene, the business places, the lives of so many people, were drastically changed! Things would never again be the same. A tragedy of this magnitude, especially in such a small town, is something that remains etched in the minds of the witnesses, never to be forgotten. The events of just one night would affect them for the rest of their lives.

Our highest hope is that both the young reader as well as the mature reader will appreciate the story told here. It is a story arising from the reminiscing of a previous generation, told time and again to the following generation, and finally collected into this book where it can be pondered and enjoyed for years to come.

Secondly we also hope that this book, and especially the photographs contained herein, give an accurate picture of the kind of fires so common in small American towns in the first part of this century, but about which so little has been told.

CONTENTS

BRADFORD, OHIO

Bradford, Ohio, circa 1915. Looking north on Miami Avenue is the heart of the business district of Bradford. This view depicts a very typical community in western Ohio -- dirt streets, two story buildings and a rustic feeling. The Bradford fire of 1920 started in the Arnold Lumber Yard on the right. *-- Bradford Public Library collection*

Bradford, Ohio, a small village sitting on the Darke-Miami County line was an important terminal on the great Pennsylvania Railroad in 1920. Boasting a population of just over 2,000 residents it was modern by any standard. The village had been founded as a construction camp in the early 1850's, when the Columbus, Piqua and Indiana Railroad was built through western Ohio.

The railroad brought unprecedented growth, turning the camp into a small town. With the coming of the second railroad, the small hamlet grew, never to look back. With the railroad the town was always on the cutting-edge, growing as the railroad and the American economy grew. At its peak the Pennsylvania Railroad maintained a stunning 85% employment of Bradford residents in the early 20th century. Massive yards, an extensive roundhouse and shop complex added

greatly to the comprehensive facilities.

In the early teens the telegraph was still the primary method for outside communication with distant towns. The railroad passenger train was the connecting link to move residents to distant towns. The railroad station and the Railway Y. M. C. A. were the centers for social activity of the growing village.

The life-style of the residents back then was different than the styles of the last half of the 20th century. The streets of town were mainly dirt, with the exception of the main streets, which had been cemented in prior years. Things like electric washing machines, air-conditioning, ease of mobility with fine automobiles were mainly fantasy dreams of some distant future. Mechanical record players were the most advanced form of home entertainment. Cooking took place over a

Closest on the right in this view, circa 1910, is the Arnold Building on the east side of Miami Avenue, on the Miami County side of Bradford. The Arnold Building, built in 1895, sheltered the Post Office, which had gone around the corner by 1920, and was destroyed in the fire. The building also housed Lower's Drug Store, Dr. P. B. Minton, Dentist and the law offices of Hall and Addington. Next is the Stahl Building, built in 1895, which held Bradford's largest mercantile, Stahl and Patty. At the time of the fire it housed A. R. Patty General Store, P. C. Katherman Confectionery and Stahl and Payne Clothing. On the second floor was the lodge for the Brotherhood of Railroad Trainmen. Today (1995) the site is occupied by a service station. The small white wagon sitting at the intersection of Main and Miami is Wish's Popcorn Wagon, which advertised popcorn, peanuts, cigars and candy. The building on the corner which was Phil Fink's mercantile and grocery was being remodeled at the time of the fire, and is today the bank. *-- Bradford Public Library collection*

wood fired cook stove in the kitchen, with its side-arm water heater, the source for hot water. Baths were usually relegated to Saturday night, in a tin wash tub placed in the middle of the kitchen floor and filled with hot water heated on the stove. Everyone used the same tub of water, a bar of lye soap, either locally made or purchased from the mercantile. Maybe a little scenting added to make the bath more acceptable. A shower was the event that took place from rain clouds. Though indoor plumbing did exist, the famous out-house was still in vogue for bathroom facilities.

It appears as though the concepts of morality were much less exploitive. Neighbors genuinely knew each other and looked out for each other. Things like spelling bees, quilting bees, picnics, traveling theatre groups and church revivals were the order of the day.

One might find the town in an almost constant haze of smoke from the locomotives. At this time railroad locomotives burned coal to create steam, the power that drove the mighty locomotives.

This view is of Miami Avenue, circa 1910, looking west at the Darke County side of the business district. All of the buildings in this photo burned to the ground in the 1920 fire. The vacant lot to the right of this picture acted as a fire break, stopping further advance of the flames. Many claim that if this lot had not been present, much of the residential area to the northwest would have been incinerated also. The awning in this photo is for Fink's mercantile. -- *Bradford Public Library collection*

The business district is centered around the intersections of Main Street and Miami Avenue. Today we might think of that area as a nice shopping mall, but back then this small area was vital to the existence of every member of the community. It was a comprehensive set of shops with about everything one might expect to find in larger towns like Greenville, Troy or Piqua. There were multiple banks, a lumber yard, drug stores where many of the drugs were blended by hand. General stores carried a broad array of merchandise, groceries and hardware, and there were confectionery stores for those with a sweet tooth; bakeries for a

It is often said that a picture is worth a thousand words -- this photograph is one of them. The Arnold Block building, built in 1893, stood at the corner of Main and Miami Streets in Bradford. Today it is the site of a filling station and convenience store. The Stahl and Patty Mercantile occupied the first floor, on the second floor was the meeting hall for the Brotherhood of Railroad Trainmen, B of RT. Note the large inviting awning opened on the front of the building, used to protect the large plate glass windows and the interior of the store from the afternoon sun. One can easily invision one's self inside the store, the aromas of fresh produce, fruits, bolts of cloth stacked on the counter, jars of candy, the oiled wooden floors and the high tin ceilings, as a merchant greeted each customer by name. About the building, the fancy work under the eaves is called iron cornice work. This type of tin-work and ornamental cast iron was widely practiced in most communities at this time. Most such items came from a vast Dayton cornice trade. The idea of ornamental iron work was a very eye pleasing effect and it gave people a commercial outlet for their artistic talents, something current architecture and constructure styles no longer recognize. Another unique aspect of this picture are the standing-seam tin roofs. The local tinsmith was generally the roofer in the town. Such roofs were very durable, needed little attention, but presented problems when the structure caught fire. In western Ohio broad use of tin roofs on both commercial and residential buildings was common. To the rear of the building is the S. E. Wise Hardware and other unidentified businesses. This area of town had concrete sidewalks and curb, but dirt streets. -- *collection Earl Landis*

In this winter view circa 1910 along Miami Avenue, the buildings in the right foreground include the Masonic Lodge, with Mildred Hall on the second floor. This was the meeting site for the Church of the Brethren at the time of the 1920 fire. The small building in the middle is Boyer & Moore Hardware. -- *Bradford Public Library collection*

wide variety of fresh cakes, pies and cookies. One had a recipe book that called for the use of a secret ingredient called ''stuff.'' The ingredient it turns out was a home grown form of yeast. There was the all-important fruit market that sold a variety of fresh fruits and produce. And meat markets, where the butcher also slaughtered the cattle, hogs and chickens in a building out back and sold the meat fresh on butchering day, a day every housewife knew well. For those railroad men needing a hair cut, there were barbers, plus the always busy photographic gallery across the street. The professional people had of-

In another view looking north along Miami Avenue we find Ora Stover's Photographic Gallery on the left. It is thought his studio was on the second floor. He sold furniture on the first floor of his building. One of Henry Ford's "tin lizzie's" is parked out front, but horse and buggy still dominate the scene for street transportation. This summertime scene shows several people on the streets of downtown Bradford. -- *collection Bradford Public Library*

fices in town; physicians, lawyers who also doubled as insurance agents, and the dentists. There were shoe stores, a dry cleaner, who employed that new chemical cleaning process known as "dry-cleaning," and a clothing store and tailor shop. There was the vital hardware store that sold everything from nails to coal stoves. The tin shops not only took care of making standing seam roofs for homes, but tinware for use in the kitchen, including cookie cutters and pie pans, also known as "tins," the lunch pails and tin cups for the railroad men. The necessary grocery stores served the town's residents and bought much of their produce locally from the farmers and gardeners.

If one was inclined for recreational activities of an adult nature, there were several cigar stores and pool rooms. The cigar stores were an outgrowth of the bakeries in town. Of course there was the furniture store, with its fine cabinet maker. The furniture store also doubled as the funeral home. Then there were the livery stables and tack shops that not only took care of the horse and buggy, but made the bridles and gear or a belt for one's pants.

The railroad men needed their all-important watches maintained, so the town had watch makers, who also maintained a shelf of jewelry and operated optical shops for those needing seeing-eye glasses.

Of course there were a variety of restaurants, boarding homes and hotels, mainly for the railroad men and travelers.

Bradford also hosted a wide selection of

Bradford sported an honest-to-gosh lamp lighter. In this circa 1910 photo, he is pushing his cart down the middle of Miami Avenue. In the background is the J. F. Erisman Bakery and Bosserman's grocery. Both were destroyed in the fire. *-- Bradford Public Library collection*

churches, all trying to save the souls of the railroad men and look out for the spiritual needs of the residents of the community. Churches were highly patronized in town. They also looked out for the social welfare of the members of the community who might be down on their luck. This was in a day before public welfare assistance. The town orbited around the railroad and the families.

1917 -- 1920

The Pennsylvania Railroad made a strong commitment to the community with its 1917 announcement of a major expansion of the classification yards, the construction of a new roundhouse and back shop and improvements to the servicing facilities for the steam locomotives.

Looking west across Miami Avenue is O. L. Boyer Groceries. It was on the Darke County side of the street and at the north end of the fire area. This circa 1910 photo shows two buck-boards in front of the Boyer business. -- *Bradford Public Library collection*

To the town this meant more jobs, full employment and a better economic outlook for the future of the town. The United States was engaged in World War I, and for the first time the railroad was under control of the Federal Government. Wages were raised by staggering amounts and added 20% to the employment ranks. For Bradford it meant an artificial sense of financial security in town. Many area newspapers carried employment ads for the railroad, seeking men to come to Bradford. Housing was scarce and the railroad offered temporary housing in the form of old box cars. Set off their wheels, small doors were cut into the sides for easy access and to provide shelter until something better could be located or built.

The new automobile was making an appearance in town. These newfangled contraptions were limited to spring and summer operations. Older folks called them "machines," and youngsters found them quite a novelty to chase, but the ultimate was a chance to ride in one.

The village had electricity, generated over in Greenville. Unlike the rural areas outside of town that would not have reliable electricity for another 20 years, the town enjoyed the benefits of electricity. The town had arc lamps to light the streets at night, and many homes had the modern convenience of electric lights.

With telephones in place for 20 years, the village proved to be a very modern community.

THE FIRE DEPARTMENTS

Because of the certainty of fire in the railroad yards, the railroad had established its own fire brigade by the 1880's. This appears to be the first formal fire department in town. Men were hired to walk the roofs of the many railroad buildings, looking for anything that could start a fire, like live cinders the locomo-

Wise's boarding house on East Main Street was a favorite sleeping spot for lay-over crewmen from the Pennsylvania Railroad. In this circa 1915 photo we see a group of railroad men loafing on the wooden front porch. It was consumed by the flames in August 1920 and was not rebuilt. -- *Scott D. Trostel collection*

The two photos on this page depict the buildings on Main Street. (Top View) Looking east from Miami Avenue, all of the buildings on the right, down to the the start of the tree line, were destroyed in the fire of 1920. The Post Office and Stover's Photographic Studio are visible about half way down. The platform on the left was used for the Bradford Civic Band and band concerts. The brick building on the left was part of Fink's mercantile. (Bottom View) Looking west on Main Street toward Miami Avenue, all of the buildings on the left were consumed in the fire. Along here were many small merchants including Porter & Stover Furniture, Tom Manaci's Fruit Store, Drees Meat Market, and the Star Theatre. *-- Scott D. Trostel collection*

tives were exhausting.

The earliest fire brigade appears to have been equipped with buckets, ladders, axes and hoses on yard engine tenders to act as early day tankers in order to get water to the fire quickly.

The fire brigade was summoned to action by a certain whistle signal from the round-house. The railroad dug fire cisterns in the yards, and it appears the village may have done the same in order to protect residential properties and provide a supply of water.

Bradford had grown to the point where it, too, needed fire protection, and the Bradford Volunteer Fire Department was brought into being. Many of the men who served on the railroad's fire brigade also served on the village fire brigade.

By the turn of the century, the railroad had added hose carts, a hose house and chemical carts. The village followed close behind. It can not be determined when the village bought its first pumper cart, but many of the local villages made such purchases between 1880

The office for the Bradford Telephone Exchange had been built by the employees of the Pennsylvania Railroad in response to the need to keep men flowing to the massive railroad yards. Over 1200 railroad men got on and off the trains every 24 hours in Bradford. This office is on the second floor of one of the buildings on the west side of Miami Avenue. The night operator, Anna Lehman, remained at the switchboard summoning outside assistance for the village until it was seen the building would be destroyed in the flames. She left her post just before the exit was cut off by the flames in the 1920 fire. *-- Bradford Public Library collection*

and 1890. These pumpers were hand-operated affairs, relying on volunteers to pull them to the fire and to also pump the gang handles. It is recorded that this kind of pumper was prone to failure, and several stopped pumping at the time of major fires in their respective communities. They were simply pushed into the flames as the volunteers stood back and watched the building burn to the ground. One such incident occurred in Fletcher when the business district of that village burned to the ground.

The receipt of new fire equipment always meant a crowd gathering at the railroad station to meet the train. In Bradford the railroad car was switched to a freight platform, and the pumper was unloaded, and paraded up Miami Avenue to the City Hall, where the village fire apparatus was housed.

Since it appears that neither the railroad nor the village had a horse-drawn steam pumper, any that were needed for a major fire, had to be brought into town by the railroad. Both Piqua and Greenville had horse-drawn steam pumpers. At differing times it appears a steam pumper was requested for

Looking north at the Railway Y.M.C.A., this facility served as the social center for Bradford from 1906 to 1931. The building was threatened by flaming debris the night of the fire in 1920.   The opposite side of the building had blistered paint. If it had not been for vigilant patrols by a hose brigade, this building would have likely been consumed in the conflagration. -- *David Oroszi Collection*

(PICTURE ON NEXT PAGE) A birds eye view of Bradford, Ohio. This rare view of the downtown Bradford area was taken from the school prior to the 1920 fire. In the center of the photo is the Arnold & Son Lumber Company. On the right is the Bradford village Hall, also home for the volunteer fire department. Unique to this building is the fire bell, mounted in the cupola atop the roof of the hose tower. Bradford had the good fortune to have both a village fire department and a railroad fire brigade. Both were used to fight the fire in August 1920, but they were not enough to stop the onslot of the flames. As the fire progressed, it moved from right to left across this photo. Most of the buildings to the left of the Arnold Lumber business were destroyed in the fire. Note the ''Mail Pouch'' tobacco billboard on the side of the brick building facing the railroad. This was an unusual application and site for the sign, since it was meant for the male passengers and railroad employees on passing trains. Unique to this photo is the new village water tank sitting in the middle of the picture. The tank is low to the ground. Other photographs show it at a much higher elevation on steel legs. Apparently it was later raised to a much higher elevation. -- *collection Earl Landis*

This view looks east toward the Railway Y.M.C.A. and the passenger terminal area along the Logansport side of the Pennsylvania Railroad. The photographer has set up his camera on Miami Avenue. The buildings on the left of the railroad were all destroyed in the fire. Visible is the back of the Arnold Lumber yard and the Iddings elevator. A westbound passenger train is departing the passenger station. This afternoon picture clearly shows the proximity of the railroad station to the fire area. Today, on the gravel drive rests a railroad caboose, the sole reminder of Bradford's heritage as a railroad town. Note in the photo, the Railway Y.M.C.A. did not face Miami Avenue, but looked east, out onto the great terminal and railroad yards. -- *collection Earl Landis*

NOLD & SON
PAINT
LUMBER & COAL YARD. HARDWARE CEMENT SEWER
S EYE VIEW BRADFORD - O.

some fires. The railroad provided a locomotive and flat car, on which the pumper was loaded. It was not unusual for the process and travel to take over an hour. By that time the fire had done its damage and the trip was more for clean-up and pumping of cooling water. Grain mills along the railroad were a favorite for use of the steam pumper.

The mutual aid of the two fire departments in Bradford appears to have been common. When the railroad experienced a major fire in the yards, they ran an engine and flat car up to Miami Avenue for the loading of village firemen, hose carts and supplies down in the railroad yards.

By 1918, the railroad had built a new hose house and reel house south of the new roundhouse. During the reconstruction of the terminal an extensive network of waterlines and hydrants was installed. It is not known when the village added fire hydrants around the residential streets of town.

In the fall of 1916 the first big fire in the town took place when the roundhouse burned. Though the walls were brick, the roof was not, and burned with great ferocity. Several locomotives were trapped inside and sustained damage. The building was demolished in 1918 to make way for a larger roundhouse.

THE ROARING TWENTIES

The great influenza epidemic hit in 1918, and people everywhere were expiring from the rapid advancement of this plague. Bradford was no different than every other town in America. The undertakers were quite busy and martial law was declared that winter, just to try and stop the spread of this European disease. The great war had put many American men on French soil to quell a rife in the German dictatorship.

Trainloads of soldiers rolled through the junction every day. It was December, Christmas time, when the epidemic hit its peak.

As the year 1919 came, the disease eased

The Railway Y.M.C.A. was the center-piece for the railroad and the village of Bradford. This view looks west, at the front of the massive building. It sat in what today is the village ''Y'' Yard Park and immediately south of the fire area, to the right of this photo. -- *Scott D. Trostel collection*

Looking east along the Indianapolis Division tracks at the Pennsylvania depot about 1900. The depot grounds stood just east of the fire area, across the track. The wooden platforms on the opposite side of the station were scorched by the intense heat. All Logansport trains were held throughout the night while the Indianapolis trains continued. According to Robert Perry, ''The Indianapolis train came in shortly after 10 o'clock and the heat was so intense that the passengers had to rush up the walk to the roundhouse [to the right of this picture] to escape the heat.'' -- *Ethan Huntzinger photo, David Oroszi collection*

off and social life in town returned with the lifting of martial law. The new roundhouse and powerhouse entered operation early that year.

Bradford was looking sharp for 1920. Contractors were building spec housing, (homes constructed without a buyer, anticipating a buyer will be located prior to its completion) all of it sold before the first ground could be broken. Bradford's wild ''Oklahoma District,'' had finally been brought under control and gambling seemed less prominent.

The Railway Y.M.C.A. had given the town a sense of pride after nearly 50 years of the reckless styles of the railroad men. Strong efforts by the churches to organize were also paying off. Bradford residents who were members of the Harris Creek Church of the Brethren, just north of town, had lost their hack service when the livery closed in 1915. Many members wanted to establish a Sunday School in town proper. This became a reality in the spring of that year.

In 1917 the Bradford Church of the Brethren was formally established. They were meeting in Mildred Hall on the Darke County side of Miami Avenue, in the path of the August 1920 fire.

This church became a strong influence in the lives of many of the railroad men at this time. It is not clearly understood why, but as revivals would be held, the newspapers reported many railroad men attending. Mildred Hall was directly across the street from the Brotherhood of Railroad Trainmen Lodge, also destroyed in the 1920 fire.

This rare photograph, taken August 26, 1917, just six months after the organization of Bradford Church of the Brethren, is promotion day for the Sunday School of the Church of the Brethren in Bradford. They were meeting on the second floor of the building behind them in the windows marked Mildred Hall. This is where the Church of the Brethren was housed at this time. Religion and a faith in Jesus were very important to the people in Bradford. This town had been full of gambling, drunkards and much darker businesses, catering to the vices of the hundreds of railroad men, who used this village as their terminal. Bradford village patriarch Nate Iddings is the elderly man with the flowing white beard in the middle of the picture. Of interest, many of the younger children are dressed in white, a number have Sunday School papers in their hands or bouquets of flowers. Most of the boys are wearing knee-pants and all of the girls have leg socks. Most of the teen-age girls have bows in their hair and appear to be wearing it up, likely due to the heat of August. Most of the adult ladies have hats or bonnets on their heads. All of the adult men are wearing suits with ties. Without a doubt the clothes these people are wearing are their ''Sunday best.'' On the first floor was S. S. Miller Hardware. It is believed the hardware store had closed before the fire. Just three years later this site would be destroyed by fire. *-- collection Bradford Church of the Brethren*

(TOP VIEW) After the fire of 1920 the Bradford Church of the Brethren moved into temporary quarters at the township building on Oakwood Street. Though the building was cramped, it served until the new church was built and opened in 1923. In this view the ladies of the church are gathered around a stack of comforters they have made for relief efforts of the church. This type of work was quite common with the church not only looking out for its members, but anyone in the community who needed aid. This was in a day before government welfare programs. **(BOTTOM VIEW)** The new Church of the Brethren structure is well under construction in the summer of 1923. This property had been low ground and very little site work was needed to prepare for the basement. Note the church bell sitting in front of the building. *-- collection Bradford Church of the Brethren*

REMEMBERING THE BRADFORD FIRE

There were two things you could count on in Bradford -- trains, and the daily rounds by the lamp lighter, to fill the fuel tanks , trim the wicks and clean the globes for each evening's use. It is doubtful these men ever gave a passing thought that the buildings up and down Miami Avenue would disappear in a dramatic fire one hot August evening in 1920. -- *Bradford Public Library collection*

Tuesday, August 3, 1920, dawned as another busy day at the railroad terminal town of Bradford. The sun bore down bright and hot through the humid air. The smoke of the locomotives hung lazily over the town. Mrs. Barnes looked out her window hoping the breeze would be carrying the smoke north so she could get out the scrub board, wash and hang out a load of clothes. Her new baby was fussy from the morning heat. The thermometer on the front of the crossing watchman's shack at Miami Avenue was already registering a very warm 84 degrees.

The town boys were already discussing a junket out to the Stillwater River for a cool dip. The usual crowd had gathered at the station platform to watch the meet of Pennsylvania passenger trains Numbers 33 and 302. It was always a busy time with two trains meeting at the same time, plus one would split and continue west as two sections. They had magnificent maroon cars with gold leaf lettering and a deep varnished finish that was mirror like. Up in the coach windows were many strange faces, but always welcome to the curious on the platform. If you walked by the diner and the door to the kitchen was open you could be swept away in the aromas of a marvelous breakfast. Jake Katherman was on the platform expecting a bag of sugar and some other items needed to make some candy. A better treat today would be a cool glass of lemonade.

Some of the town youngsters had already found cool shade trees to stay under while playing or just watching the activity of the trains. Young Joe Stephens looked up to see several locomotive firemen walking to the roundhouse and he puzzled why they were dressed in coveralls and long sleeve shirts on such a hot day. Of course it was protection from the intense heat of the locomotive cab.

Up at the Y.M.C.A. the porch was filled with railroad men loafing, and a few napping,

A typical August afternoon in Bradford would find the horse-drawn water wagon sprinkling the streets to settle the dust. Note the wagon driver atop the wooden water barrel, his crutch tied to the side. Such was the slower paced life in this railroad town at the time of the Bradford fire. -- *Scott D. Trostel collection*

Looking north on South Miami Avenue at the Church Street intersection in Bradford, we find a quaint tree lined street, typical for most small towns. In this spring time picture, all seems orderly in anticipation of the coming leaves, flowers, back yard gardens and the greening of the grass. -- *Scott D. Trostel collection*

just in from runs or awaiting the call boy to summon them for another train out. Over in the flower beds, Sando Fontana was trying to keep the exquisite gardens watered and to find a spot in the shade as the sun rose higher in the sky.

Young Johnny Layer and Delmar Faun had reported to their jobs at the Y.M.C.A. knowing a big crowd of railroad men would be patronizing their pool tables in the cool basement of the ''Y.'' With the newly enlarged railroad yards it hardly seemed like the ''Y'' was big enough to hold all the men coming and going around the terminal.

Later that day a few of the neighbor ladies, having a back yard conversation at the fence, were heard to say it would be a sticky night to try and sleep. The breeze might stop when the sun set. One had even commented that they had turned the summer porch into a bedroom for the kids. With the constant smoke and all, it would be tough trying to drift into dream land.

Even a hot sticky evening was a welcome relief from a humid August day. The ten hour work days in the yards or roundhouse could sure drain a fellow of any ambition. Many of the railroaders and their families had taken to sitting a spell on the front porch just to escape the heat of the house as the sun dropped off in the west as a big orange ball. This time of year the night trick at the railroad was the desired time for work.

Catherine Bazill was a well known cook at the Railway Y.M.C.A. She resided on Main Street and would be getting off work at 10:00 P.M., in time to see her children before it was time for bed. Her daughter Lillian, recalls that night, ''Everything was quiet as usual when Mom came home...'' Some of her six kids always walked over to meet her coming out of the ''Y'' every night, just to enjoy her company during the walk back to their home.

Johnny Layer and Delmar Faun were getting off work from the Railway Y.M.C.A. that evening, commenting on how busy it had been. They headed out to Miami Avenue and up toward Main Street on the darkened sidewalk. The heat of the day still radiated up and it was just too sticky to think about sleeping. The usual sounds of locomotive exhausts, a few short whistle blasts and the coupling of cars pierced the night, only accented by the crickets. In just a few short minutes their lives and the lives of most residents of Bradford would be changed dramatically. As they walked by the Arnold Lumber Company gate on North Miami Avenue they smelled the strong scent of Kerosene and looked in to see the first flames. Immediately the two ran south of the "Commons" and sounded the alarm bell for the fire department.

By the time the first volunteer firemen arrived, the fire had broken through the roof. Of immediate danger was the telephone exchange, located in the Masonic Lodge building across the street. The building was just five years old. From there one of the operators, Anna Lehman, manned the switch board to summon out of town help until near 11:00 P.M. that night. She left her post just minutes before the exit was cut off by flames. It seemed like the entire village was awakened by the cries of those at the scene of the blaze where true realization of the danger confronting the village was seen. Many residents risked life and limb to save their homes and businesses until exhausted in their efforts.

The fire worsened rapidly and the railroad summoned its fire brigade into action bringing hoses, ladders and making their water supplies available. The railroad was forced to close the Logansport mainline for over four hours. The Pennsy sent rescue trains out to several local towns to bring fire equipment and manpower back to help fight the fire. The vicious gains of the fire brought a response from fire departments at Piqua, Versailles and Covington. They were able to do little to stop the flames. Chief Caulfield of the Piqua Fire Department took charge of all on scene operations. The firemen were greatly hampered by an inadequate water supply. The *Greenville Daily Tribune* attributed the lack of water as a large cause for the extra heavy losses experienced by the local businesses. The Greenville Fire Department was called, but the fire reached the phone lines as the call was being completed and the message did not get through until later, when it was delivered as a message from the railroad.

As the flames spread eastward on Main Street, many frightened families there began moving personal belongings out of their homes. Recalling how close the fire came to their home, Lillian Bazill Baughman said, "Our house was next!" Friends and neighbors helped the Bazill family move their furniture out and across the street into the yard of neighbor Harry Allen. Although fire did spare their house, the adjoining property burned to the ground.

Trying to save their goods, merchants were dragging much into the streets where it was piled. As the fire advanced it had to be picked up and carried away again. In a number of instances stocks were removed to a temporary place of safety only to have it destroyed later when the fire reached it. Practically all of the merchandise in the village was destroyed and immediate pleas went out for assistance.

When the telephone exchange burned, all public telephone service was cut off and the railroad became the only source for outside communications. The radiated heat was so intense that the paint started to blister on the Y.M.C.A. some distance away, and a fire brigade was assigned to hose it down. There a couple of fellows walked the roof watching for hot embers, which showered down most of the night. On three separate occasions flames erupted on the building. They were quickly extinguished before fire could erupt on a third front.

The fire jumped west across Miami Avenue and started burning the business block north of the railroad, but the many brick structures in that area finally slowed the gain. Young Harry Royer had a good view of the fire, having sneaked into the partially remodeled Bradford National Bank building. He stood in the stone window opening watching the buildings burn until the heat became too intense, then he would sit under the window opening to cool off for a few minutes.

Town folks feared that the uncontrolled fire would engulf the entire village and many residents gathered personal belongings and got out of town. One little girl thought about what she wanted to take when her father came home and announced that they should leave. She gathered up her two new kittens and cradled them in her arms while they walked down the street. When they got in the vicinity of the fire the kittens jumped down and ran off never to be seen again.

Members of the American Legion took up arms to guard against looting with the mass of merchandise in the streets. The next morning the destruction was quite evident.

The great fire that swept through the business district of Bradford, destroyed 34 businesses and 12 residences. The shock was all too real and Bradford had lost a major portion of its business district. Included in the losses were:

(Kuntz) Arnold & Son Lumber
First National Bank
Lower's Drug Store
A. R. Patty General Store
Brotherhood of Railroad Trainmen
* Lodge*
P. C. Katherman Confectionery
U. S. Post Office
C. E. Walter Barber Shop
Porter & Stover Furniture
Ora Stover Photograph Gallery
C. E. Livingston Pool Room

Tom Manaci Fruit Store
Star Theatre
McDonald "Mack's" Meat Market
Arnold & Iddings Elevator
Westerville Cream Station
Dr. G. W. Bausman Office and Resi-
* dence*
Albert Wise Boarding House and Resi-
* dence*
L. E. Harvey Law Office
Coppock Bros. Meat Market
Moore's Hardware Store
Mauck's Milk Depot
George Drees Meat Market
John Zimmerman Barber Shop
S. F. McCarty's Shoe Store and Dry
* Cleaning*
O. L. Boyer Grocery
J. F. Erisman Bakery
Stahl and Payne Clothing
Boyer and Moore Hardware
Hudson Pool Room
Parin & Blizzard Tin Shop
L. E. Carver Residence
Fred Durr Residence
Masonic Temple
Telephone Exchange
Red Men's Hall
C. E. Livingston Residence
Edward Dye Pool Room
Seven apartments over the businesses
Twenty five freight cars of the Penn-
* sylvania Railroad*

A good portion of these businesses were located in the Iddings Block and were not insured by Nate Iddings, owner. He never rebuilt the structures, but instead donated the land as a small park. Losses were estimated at better than $1,000,000.00.

Over the days following, the roads into town were literally clogged with sightseers. Many reporters and photographers from distant cities came to file reports, but owing to the great destruction practically all restaurants and eating places were destroyed and many were going hungry. When they realized the suffering of the many local residents, they offered money in order to help get premises cleaned up and households back in order.

The Red Cross sent a volunteer team to render aid and assistance with clothing and shelter for the homeless. The Piqua and Greenville telephone companies sent linemen to help get the mass of downed phone wires back in order and service restored.

The day after the fire Claude Payne of the firm of Stahl and Payne Clothing died from shock after learning that his business had been destroyed. He was attending the funeral of a friend in Greenville at the time the news was delivered. He carried almost no insurance on the business. His death was the only one recorded as a result of the fire.

The bank vault survived and was opened after it had cooled sufficiently, to reveal cash, notes and bank records unharmed.

It was not until August 6th, three days after the fire, that the clean-up and demolition of the remaining walls could begin. The Brotherhood of Railroad Trainmen moved right across the street and built a new building next to the bank. At the time of the fire the bank was undergoing extensive renovation including a new facade. Patty once more took up business on the first floor of the B of RT Hall. Most businesses never reopened.

The Deputy State Fire Marshal immediately started an investigation of the scene to determine whether the cause was arson or from another cause. A number of volunteers who arrived at the scene of the fire within the Arnold Lumber Yard were interviewed. The official cause was listed as arson, though the perpetrator could not be discovered. Four other fires were reported in a four week period of time prior to the fire, all at the Arnold Lumber Company, and all were caught in time to prevent serious damage. Arson was strongly suspected in a follow-up investigation of those fires.

HEADLINES FROM AREA NEWSPAPERS

THE PIQUA DAILY CALL AUGUST 4, 1920

BRADFORD PRACTICALLY WIPED OUT

TROY DAILY NEWS AUGUST 4, 1920

BRADFORD IS SWEPT BY MILLION DOLLAR FIRE THAT DESTORYS PART OF BUSINESS SECTION OF COMMUNITY....

THE GREENVILLE DEMOCRAT AUGUST 4, 1920

DISASTEROUS FIRE VISITS BRADFORD

GREENVILLE DAILY TRIBUNE AUGUST 4, 1920

BUSINESS SECTION OF BRADFORD ALMOST WIPED OUT BY FIRE

DAYTON DAILY NEWS AUGUST 4, 1920

PROBE $1,000,000 BRADFORD FIRE

THE DAYTON JOURNAL HERALD AUGUST 5, 1920

BLAZE SWEEPS BRADFORD

(ABOVE) Probably along East Main Street, all that remains are fragments of walls, twisted pipes and ashes. Most of the retail merchant business district was gone in a matter of hours. -- *D. Faun photo, S. Trostel collection*

(PREVIOUS PAGE) This is the sight which greeted Bradford residents on the morning of August 4, 1920, massive destruction along East Main Street. Witnesses found a business district in total ruin -- by fire. -- *D. Faun photo, S. Trostel collection*

This view looks east from along the railroad on the Darke County side of the fire area. This skeleton is probably the remains of Mildred Hall and the Masonic Lodge. On the extreme left in the background is the new First National Bank building. The bank was not yet open, having occupied space in the Arnold block just down the street. Their facility was destroyed but records were saved in the vault, which when the fire cooled, was opened. The records were moved to the new building which was opened in weeks after the fire.
--D. Faun photo, S. Trostel collection

INTERVIEWS OF THE WITNESSES

Several of the residents were interviewed to get their recollections of the fire. The first, Adelaide Tyler Wilson, who was thirteen at the time, had this to say: ''Word went around to get anything you wanted to keep because you might get burned out.'' She loaded up her three tiger cats and left the house with her folks. The cats' fear of the fire caused them to flee her arms, and they were never seen again. ''My sister Ruth, took her junior-senior reception dress. People took their things out north of Bradford. When the fire was over, there were a lot of things they couldn't find. Looters had been there.''

Her father had been called out to a train wreck and wasn't home at the time the fire started. ''They were all excited and sad.'' Adelaide stated, ''It was hard for people to build back up, a lot of them couldn't afford it.''

She stated, ''The bank vault stayed hot four days, but everything inside was fine.''

Seventeen year old Opal Katherman Patty was was dating her future husband, George Patty. She stated, ''At the time of the fire I was living with my parents, Jacob (Jake) and

35

This is the southeast corner of Main and Miami Avenue in Bradford on the morning of August 4, 1920. The Arnold block is completely gone. Compare this photo to the same view on page 10. The Stahl & Patty mercantile is in complete ruins. It is reported that the merchants, including Patty and Katherman moved their stock of merchandise into the street as a protection from potential loss by fire. The flames moved so quickly, fed by a wind from the southeast, their buildings and most of their inventory was destroyed. -- *Scott D. Trostel collection*

(TOP PHOTO NEXT PAGE) Moving down the Arnold block is the remains of the First National Bank. The door of the vault is on the right. The vault room was made of concrete and protected the records, cash and securities from destruction. It is said it took a week for the door and walls to cool sufficiently before they could be opened. Note the Railway Y.M.C.A. in the right background. (BOTTOM PHOTO NEXT PAGE) A week after the fire the vault was opened. In the door are packages of currency destined for the payroll of the hundreds of railroad men, as well as bank records and securities. Three of the six men in the photo are identified. The two fellows on the left are unknown. Harry Royer is sitting in the doorway. The man on the right is Forest Dwyer, the man standing with his hand on his waist is unknown. The man on the right is Ray Porter. -- *Bradford Public Library collection*

36

This view looks south across Main Street near the intersection of Clay Street. In the foreground are the ashen remains of the Iddings elevator and some residential homes. In the background are piles of burning grain and glowing piles of lumber and coal from the Arnold Lumber Company. The building on the right appears to be part of the Arnold Block. Though the fire started in the Arnold Lumber buildings, it burned in two directions, east and west, jumping Miami Avenue and consuming most of the commercial buildings on the Darke County side of the village. *-- Vaughn Kniesly collection*

Catherine Katherman, brothers Jerry, Paul and sisters, Llora and Ethel on a farm on State Route 721 a mile north of Bradford.''

George had driven his truck out to get Opal during the evening. They were going to a medicine show in the Oakdale part of Bradford on that Tuesday. ''For some reason we went back to his home and took my fathers car home, parking it in front of the house when we heard the fire whistle blow.'' The fire whistle was at the railroad roundhouse. The town survived by the talk of that whistle. A certain sequence of short and long blows gave meaning to some event at the railroad. The worst calls were for fire and train wrecks.

She continues, ''We walked out to where we could see, and there we saw the whole sky lit up! We didn't tell my parents. The fire was burning pretty strong and George took off and that was the last I saw of him for two or three days. He went to Patty's store to help his Dad. The store had a ladder that was on a track and George was trying to get everything off the shelves that he could.''

After the fire George moved to another site across the street and reopened for business. The store remains in operation today.

Bill Elson was living up on School Street at the time of the fire. He was working for the Pennsylvania Railroad, PRR. His recollections were vivid. ''I was in town from a run at the time of the fire, burning shingles were

Looking south into the smoke at the intersection of Main and Miami Avenue, there is little anyone could do but count their losses, and thank God no one was hurt or killed in the fire. Barely visible in the right is a ladder, abandoned by one of the fire departments. Witnesses report the fire spread so rapidly there was no opportunity for the fire departments to establish a good fire line. -- *Vaughn Kniesly collection*

blowing up over our house. The wind was blowing from the east. I was working second trick on the railroad. It was 11 o'clock and I got off at 11. I came right up by that lumber yard. I didn't see any fire and when I got home up on School Street that blaze was coming up over us.''

Bill continues, ''The fire was set! Nobody

could tell me different...When I went by the lumber yard on the way home I didn't smell any smoke. No, I never went back down town, I watched it from my own place. I remember when Versailles burned. I was just a real little kid then, the folks lived in Web-ster, and that's about three miles.''

When asked about the town gossip fol-lowing the fire, Bill offered some comments. ''You heard all kinds of stories... It was blamed mostly on a fellow that worked there [at the lumber yard.] He's dead now, and most of his family is gone from around here. He was blamed for a lot of it.''

Some of the towns folks thought the sus-pect had quit or been fired before the fire, but Elson explains, ''It was while he was working there. He lived in town.''

Elson suggested the business practices

The unidentified photograph on East Main Street is thought to be the residence of and office for Dr. Bausman. Note the remains of the front porch and steps. The spoked wheel set is that of a hose cart, either belonging to the Bradford Fire Department or the Pennsylvania Railroad Fire Brigade. It is impossible to imagine the panic that went through the town that fateful night or the sense of loss at seeing businesses, inventories and homes destroyed in such a horrible manner. -- *Lucile Dedrick collection*

BRADFORD PRACTICALLY WIPED OUT

followed by the Arnold Lumber Company may have been suspect and caused a great deal of hard feelings in the community.

Elson went on to make a few other comments about the fire, ''The whole square burnt clear over to Main Street, all the way down to Doc Bausman's house. There were some frame buildings up this way...just too close to the lumber yard. The lumber yard was set right along the railroad. It was a frame building, clear up front [to Miami Avenue.] The brick buildings were north of it on Main Street -- the Post Office was in there, Patty's store, Doc Bausman's doctor's office. On the west side [of Miami Avenue,] ... there

was a three story building in there, Mildred Hall, the Masonic Lodge, Boyer's Grocery...''

When asked how he thought the fire effected the village he responded, ''The only thing that really held us here was the railroad.''

THE DAYS FOLLOWING THE
FIRE

Blanche Kniesly recalls how everyone in their house was surprised to find out about the fire the following morning; everyone, that is, except her grandfather. At the time of the fire Blanche was still at home with her par-

Just west of Dr. Bausman's home is another view on Main Street. The destruction by fire is absolute! Looking at this photo and imagining being there, one can feel both the heat of the August morning sun and the radiated heat from the glowing embers of the fire. The acrid smell of the smoke would tend to make an impression on anyone, and it would not soon be forgotten. Today we might ask ourselves if the fire would have been equally destructive if all of the modern fire fighting technology were available. We don't know the answer, but such fires would challenge the wits of any fire department. -- *Vaughn Kniesly collection*

ents, Bert and Mary Elizabeth Frey, and her grandfather, Samuel Magee. Their family farm was located two miles east of Bradford on the north side of what is now Covington Bradford Road.

That morning, Blanche's brother and sister-in-law, Earl and Fay Frey, came by train from their home in Piqua after they heard the news about Bradford. When they got to the farm, they discovered that Blanche and her parents knew nothing of the great fire.

But grandfather already knew! Apparently Samuel had gotten up sometime during the night, had looked out a west window, and had seen the blaze in the night sky. Conclud-

ing that there was nothing he or anyone else could do, he simply went back to bed, not saying a word to anyone. Only when Earl and Fay happened to come by did Samuel reveal that he had seen the fire.

The newspapers gave dramatic coverage to the fire and the personal tragedy of the residents. Many of the articles were written not only to describe the scene, but the struggles and hardships of the residents.

Here are a few excerpts from the *Piqua Daily Call* for August 4, 1920. ''The actual loss to the buildings alone is near $400,000 and it is estimated that less than one-third this amount was carried in insurance, largely for

This photograph shows an unidentified block wall standing somewhere along East Main Street. The view looks north from along the railroad. The site is immediately east of Miami Avenue. No property maps of the sites exist that show the abutting properties at the time of the fire. It is thought the railroad track may have been the siding for Arnold Lumber and the remaining wall could be from the Iddings building. It appears the First National Bank is on the left background of the photo. -- *Lucile Dedrick collection*

the reason that a high rate was demanded because of the lumber yard and buildings being located in the heart of the business district.

''Near eleven o'clock when it was seen the village was entirely at the mercy of the seething flames, telephone calls for help were sent to Piqua, Gettysburg, Covington, Versailles and similar towns...

''...In an hour all of the equipment called for was at the scene and then the water gave out leaving the visiting firemen, under the direction of Chief P. J. Caulfield of the Piqua department, to fight the flames with nerve alone ... The visitors lent valuable aid not to be doubted because the good people of Brad-

A similar view from that of page 36 finds a mother and two youngsters surveying the scene the next morning. Looking east there is nothing left but a hot pile of ashes and the memories of people who had patronized the merchants. It is very apparent once the flames had gone out of control, that only a miracle could keep the rest of the town from being incinerated. Such destructive fires were not uncommon in small towns. In the local area Versailles, Fletcher and St. Paris all witnessed the destruction of their business areas due to fires. -- *Lucile Dedrick collection*

ford, down hearted and saddened by the terrible loss they faced, gave many expressions of satisfaction for what was done by the visiting departments ... To Chief Caulfield they all pay a high tribute for the work he directed and for his method employed in combating the blaze.''

The crowds that came to town in the following days were so large that traffic officers were stationed at many intersections to prevent congestion and collisions. Parking along the fire area was prohibited.

Nate Iddings, by 1920 an elderly man, decided not to rebuild the buildings in his block. He gave it to the community of Bradford as a park and Public Square.

J. C. Erisman purchased the site of the Masonic Lodge and immediately commenced

This rare photograph shows part of the inventory and display cases from one of the mercantiles setting in the middle of the street. It is hard to imagine these store owners rushing to save their goods, having the presence to enter buildings in danger of fire or maybe even being on fire as they continued hasty efforts to try and save part of their goods. This was in a day when the benefit of insurance was not widely relied upon and trust in insurance was still not widely known. The two gentlemen in the photograph appear to be stunned and amazed by the scenes of destruction before their eyes. No doubt they knew most of the store owners and residents affected by the fire. -- *Vaughn Kniesly collection*

HELP THE NEEDY IN BRADFORD

Rev. C. S. Grauser announced at the Chatauqua Wednesday night at the request of the Piqua Daily Call and Press-Dispatch that on Thursday evening between the performances a collection will be taken for the relief of the sufferers from the Bradford fire. It is hoped that $500 or more will be collected.

Everyone is asked to contribute something and in order that every Piquad will have the chance to give the office of the Call has been made headquarters for the collection, where contributions be received until Saturday at noon.

Saturday afternoon Mayor J. H. Smith and a committee will be sent to Bradford with the funds and they will be turned over to the mayor of Bradford and a committee to be distributed among the sufferers.

Person who benefited by the gifts sent from Bradford during the flood are especially urged to contribute to the gift of Piquads to Bradford citizens.   (Piqua Daily Call 8/5/1920)

AN EDITORIAL PLEA IN THE *PIQUA DAILY CALL*

August 5, 1920

Lend a Helping Hand

During the dark days following the terrible flood of 1913 when Piquads hungered and when they were cold, the good people of Bradford realizing that assistance was highly necessary in order to prevent actual suffering, packed a car load of provisions, bed-clothing and fresh dairy products and dispatched the life saving shipment to this city. Children and grown-ups were given food and the amount of good that this car load did is not to be reckoned in words or figures.

Bradford people were not asked for food for the hearts of Piquads were too sore and too full of sorrow to think of aid when the awful significance of the flood was before them occupying their every thought and staggering them with its magnitude.

Bradford today is suffering from the effects of a calamity as great in its scope and as fearful to that village as the flood was to Piqua and surely Piquads will not even have to be asked to contribute to a fund to be raised but only notified that a fund is being raised for the relief of those families and merchants who lost their all in the fire Tuesday night.

Returning the gift of Bradford villagers of flood times is a privilege that Piquads will not overlook and the purse strings of all should be opened wide to help those who helped us when we were in dire distress. It is hoped that five hundred or more dollars will be received to be distributed by a committee to those in Newberry township who need help and who will accept aid from Piqua citizens who accepted aid from Bradford when personal pride and feeling was discarded through the stern necessities brought about by calamity.

Persons will have the opportunity to give to the cause at the Chatauqua tonight. If you cannot be there appoint a friend to drop your money in the box but let every man and woman in the city contribute something and repay with tenfold interest the debt of gratitude that is owed to Bradford citizens.

At the corner of Main and Miami Avenue is a Model T Touring car with a trailer. It might have been driven in by a village resident in an effort to help move goods and inventory away from the fire or the furniture of one of the residents? It is apparent the car had been there in the height of the fire; it is covered with fly ash. Onlookers seem to be in a state of stunned disbelief as they look over the remains of the buildings. It is apparent the firemen faced many hazards during their battle that night. Collapsed walls, falling power lines and intense heat were just a few of the dangers. -- *Lucile Dedrick collection*

A letter from Bradford Mayor J. W. Routson to Chief P. J. Caulfield, Piqua Fire Department

My Dear Chief:

Please accept our heart felt thanks for your service and words of cheer during the late conflagration.

It is certainly gratifying to think of the sacrifice that you and your men made in our behalf and we will be willing to return the favor so far as we are able to do so any time the opportunity may occur.

Respectfully yours,
J. W. ROUTSON
Mayor

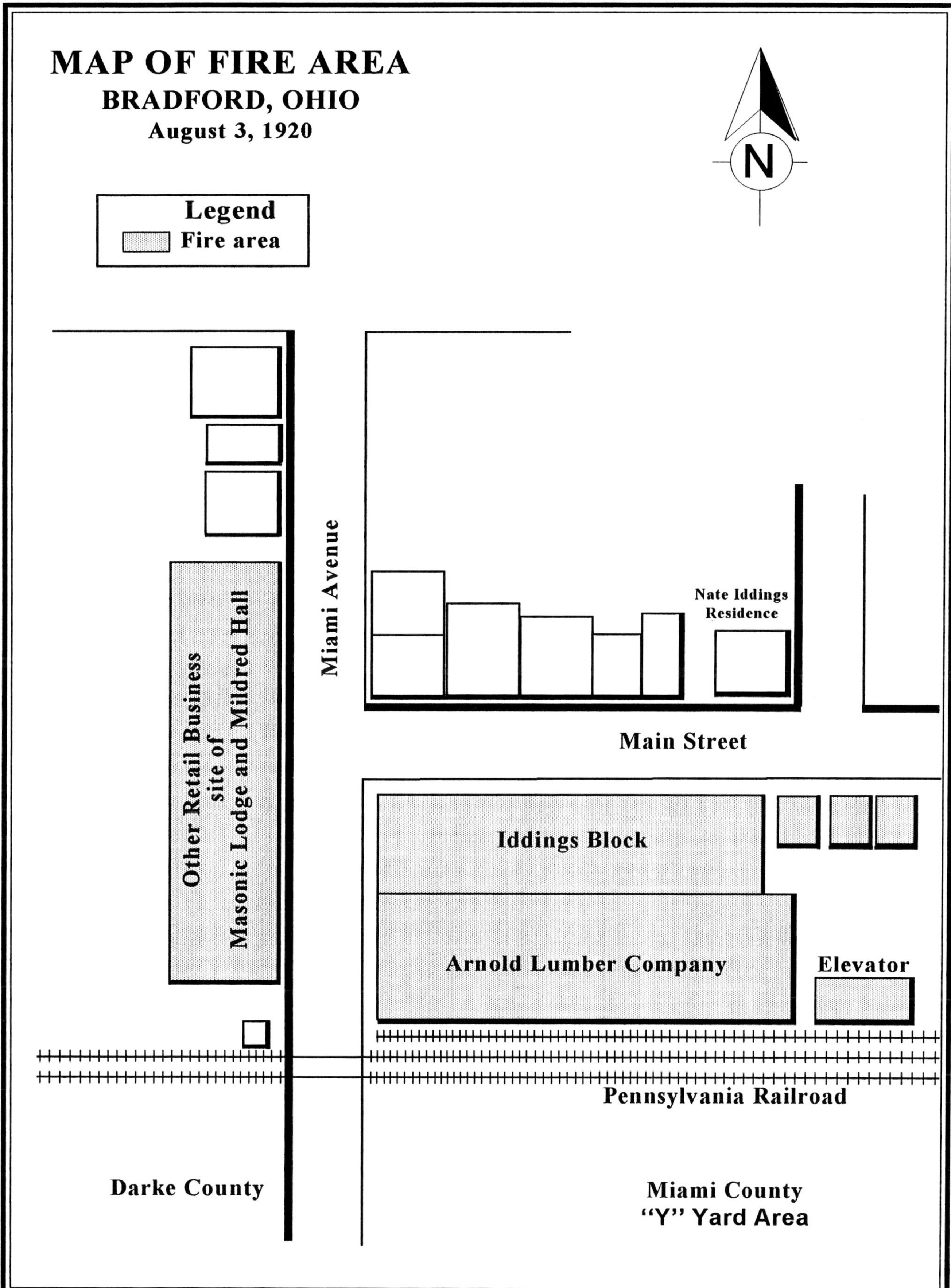

MAP OF FIRE AREA
BRADFORD, OHIO
August 3, 1920
N
Legend
Fire area
Miami Avenue
Other Retail Business
site of
Masonic Lodge and Mildred Hall
Nate Iddings
Residence
Main Street
Iddings Block
Arnold Lumber Company
Elevator
Pennsylvania Railroad
Darke County
Miami County
"Y" Yard Area

Looking south on Miami Avenue at the massive destruction on the west side (Darke County side) of the street, all of the businesses are in total ruin. It is difficult to tell which of these shells housed the Church of the Brethren and Mildred Hall. A lady stands amid the ruins, as if hoping to find some lost possession. Others stand in the right center of the photograph. This is a stark reminder of our fragile exist-ence. *-- Lucile Dedrick collection*

the work of cleaning it up in preparation for rebuilding. M. L. Boyer purchased the shell to the north and the Masonic Lodge announced it would relocate to the second floor of both buildings once construction was completed.

While work started on the building on the west side of Miami Avenue, the State Fire Marshal maintained an intensive investigation for causes of the fire in the Arnold Lumber buildings ashes. Assisted by Mayor J. W. Routson and village Fire Chief Roscoe W.

Inman, they first called all the witnesses together for intensive interviews. It was discovered that this was the fourth such fire of a suspicious nature at the lumber yard in four weeks. D. R. Faun reported he smelled the strong scent of coal-oil at the time he was passing the lumber yard. It was confirmed by several others and was the basis for determining arson as the cause.

Through August 6th the fire area remained guarded by the American Legion Post in Brad-

The only building not destroyed in the blaze was the railroad crossing watchman's shanty on the west side of Miami Avenue. No doubt the watchman was quite busy, guarding the crossing that night. His job changed from the usual protection of pedestrian and buggy traffic, to hold trains back for the passage of fire equipment. It is likely that at least part of the out-of-town fire equipment arrived by rail that evening. US 36 was not paved for another three years.
-- Scott D. Trostel collection

ford. They maintained their guard until the investigation was completed and the bank vault opened and emptied.

REBUILDING THE BUSINESS DISTRICT

At a special town meeting on August 5th, it was unanimously decided to rebuild the business district as rapidly as possible. The early indication was that financial resources would be made available to assist in the clean-up and reconstruction process.

The phones were back in operation by August 10th in a temporary office established at Arnold's new lumber yard on Oakwood Street in the Darke County side of town.

Arnold's noted they had plenty of building materials on hand and an ample supply on the way to satisfy most building needs. The telephone switchboard was being shipped in by

Standing on Miami Avenue at the entrance to the walkway for the passenger depot, one can see the smoldering remains the next morning. The fire hoses were laid under the railroad tracks so they would not be cut up under the wheels of passing train traffic. Many of the railroad ties in this area burned during the fire and the rail was heat warped. The railroad claimed damage to several freight cars which were apparently stored on the siding near the concrete wall. This was the scene that greeted passengers on passing trains the next morning. -- *Scott D. Trostel collection*

rail and would be located on the second floor of the Community Store at the corner of School Street and Miami Avenue.

A. R. Patty's store was opened in the front bay of the fire department, taking care of customers by personally calling on each patron since no local phone service was available.

Boyer and Moore Hardware purchased A.

L. Wade's stock of hardware and tools and relocated beside the Hamilton Shoe Store. They estimated it would be about a week until they would be fully stocked. Mack's Butcher Shop relocated to a room behind his restaurant on the north side of Main Street.

Porter and Stover, operators of the Bradford Furniture Store had no immediate relocation plans but maintained they would try to

Standing on the railroad station platform the vastness of the fire damage is apparent. This view looks west. The remains of the buildings are clouded in smoke. Note the railroad's telegraph lines laying on the hedge row. This clearly indicates that the Logansport Division of the railroad was without telegraph service until new poles could be set and copper line re-strung. The pole line was to the north side of the railroad track against the buildings. -- *Lucile Dedrick collection*

reopen soon.

The newspapers reported the finest sort of spirit prevailed and everybody was lending a helping hand to the sufferers of the disaster. The reporter in the *Bradford Sentinel* reported, ''We have a mighty fine community after all.''

A LITTLE KNOWN FACT

For 75 years history has stated it was Arnold Lumber that burned on the night of August 3, 1920. The lumber yard had, in fact, recently been purchased by the Peter Kuntz Lumber Company of Dayton, Ohio. Arnold's Lumber had moved into a bigger yard at the corner of High and Oakwood streets, two

The underexposure of this photograph gives emphasis to the terrible nature of fire. This view looks west from the west end of the passenger station walkway. The hedge row gives the appearance of a black wall. -- *Vaughn Kniesly collection*

blocks west. Because John T. Arnold had only recently sold his old yard on Miami Avenue, it remained known as Arnold's Lumber, though he was no longer the owner. Enjoying his larger yard, apparently itself under some phase of construction at the time of the fire, it contained several sheds, but lacked the facilities of a complete office, though it appears to have been mostly finished.

Arnold's old yard had become cramped and they sought larger facilities because Bradford was experiencing a building boom at the time.

The unanswered question will always remain; why was this fire set? It remains a mystery. Was someone angry with the Arnolds and did not know they had sold their old yard? Was someone trying to get at the new owners, Kuntz Lumber? Was a real fire bug on the loose who got some thrill out of setting fires? The investigation never turned up a clear suspect though several were pointed out as possibly being involved in the plot.

In later years Arnold sold his new lumber yard to Peter Kuntz. Kuntz could be seen

Looking to the northwest along the passenger station walkway, this photograph shows the emptiness where the Arnold & Iddings Elevator stood just the day before. The big pipe is a stand-pipe used to fill the water tender of passing steam locomotives. The man on the extreme right is a railroad section-hand. At this location on the railroad, the tracks had smooth wooden platforms so that passengers could easily walk to the trains. The west end of this platform was burned and the railroad men are likely working on removing the remains of burned plank timbers. -- *Vaughn Kniesly collection*

traveling over the streets of Bradford in his sixteen cylinder Cadillac, on his way to over see the business.

As a postscript to the Arnold Lumber story, PK Lumber eventually closed their lumber yard and mill in Bradford. In June of 1976 the buildings burned to the ground in another unsolved arson fire.

WHAT THE TOWN BECAME

Bradford entered the twentieth century as a most progressive community, whose destinies were determined by a single enterprise - - the Pennsylvania Railroad. Looking back, who'd ever thought...

After the turn of the century the railroad was growing at such a rapid pace that the

This view looks west into the burned out shell of Mildred Hall. On the walls are the twisted steel beams. In the center of the far wall is the twisted fire escape. The balance of the walls have fallen inside the structure. By 1923 this building was completely rebuilt as a two-story structure. It remains standing today on the west side of Miami Avenue. -- *Bradford Public Library collection*

yards would one day stretch for over two miles, or that the yards would be abandoned in 1929, just ten years after their massive expansion.

The town was so prosperous entering the 1920's that it boasted two banks and a savings and loan association.

It all started slipping in 1920. The fire was the first of several adverse events thrust upon the town. In 1922 the shopcraft unions of the railroad went on strike. The community was split apart by the loyalists and the scabs as the bitter strike went forward.

Over the next few years railroad men found their jobs abolished or transferred to distant cities.

It was October 29, 1929, when word reached the town that all terminal operations on the railroad would cease. It was awful news at the worst possible time. Soon the once busy yards were closed. Railroad men were transferred out or lost their jobs. The massive yards, completed in 1919 were closed and were used to hold old and unneeded cars

Newly completed First National Bank building at the corner of Miami and Main Streets in Bradford during 1920. To the rear is the new Patty's Mercantile under construction. The Brotherhood of Railroad Trainmen's Hall located to the second floor when the building was finished. Patty's is still in the same building today. The B of RT closed about 1930 and dissolved their local lodge when the Pennsylvania Railroad closed the terminal activities. It is reported that many a fine oyster supper and dance was held by the B of RT.
-- Bradford Public Library collection

and surplus locomotives, stored awaiting sale to a scrapper. The yards sat silent for another 25 years before being dismantled in the late 1950's.

In 1931 the Railway Y.M.C.A. closed. The gem of Bradford ceased with the insult and sterility of a public auction. The once beautiful building and grounds fell into neglect as the Great Depression turned more ominous. The building was salvaged for its lumber. Some of the beautiful marble was removed and reused in the entrance of the Bradford city building.

Bradford Building and Loan closed. Many of the homes they held mortgages on were abandoned by owners. Most of these families

Here is the photograph of the new telephone switchboard. It was being installed on the second floor in the back of the Community Store. This business was originally located on the southwest corner of School Street and Miami Avenue. By the middle of September 1920, it was in operation with local phone service restored. *-- Bradford Public Library collection*

had fathers, husbands or other families members laid off by the railroad. Some residents simply packed up and moved away in search of work, abandoning all hope for a revival of the railroad.

There were many hurt feelings towards the railroad that had once been the provider of jobs and income to the community.

Unfortunately, many of the towns leadership moved away as the jobs left with the railroad.

The trains rolled through every day. And they stopped for coal and water, but no crews were changed. A few machinists worked a couple of tracks over in the roundhouse. The station still had an agent and clerks. The tower had its operators and there were track gangs, but only a fraction of the number once employed there.

At the end of WW I Bradford embraced a new technology -- aircraft production. A few planes were assembled in one of the railroad stores department buildings on South Miami Avenue. The venture was not successful.

Aerial view of the fire area about three years after the fire. In the foreground is the empty lot that Nate Iddings gave to the village as a park. On the corner the P & T Oil Compny Service Station has taken the place of Katherman's. The basement and vault of the old bank remain unfilled at this date. The wooden platform behind the basement area is the band stand. Many concerts were held there. The bank located to its new white stone building at the intersection of Miami Avenue and Main Street in this photograph, where it remains in operation yet today. On the left (west) of Miami Avenue, most of the buildings in the foreground are newly rebuilt. Portions of the walls not heavily damaged in the fire were repaired and used when reconstruction of those facilities commenced. The stark early spring landscape is quite evident in this photograph. *-- collection Bradford Public Library*

BRADFORD TODAY

An aerial view of Bradford, Ohio about 1955. The view is looking east, toward Covington, Ohio. The street to the left of the railroad is Main Street, the abandoned railroad yards are still visible in the distance. *-- Scott D. Trostel collection*

During the 1920's Nate Iddings proposed the construction of a commercial airport on eighty acres of ground just east of town in conjunction with the proposed airplane-train airmail service being proposed by the Pennsylvania Railroad. His offer was rejected by the railroad and instead an air field was used on the east side of Columbus for the new service.

As any town with courage, the hurts were swallowed and the people forged ahead, finding ways to overcome the many destructive forces thrust upon them in just 20 short years. With the onset of WW II local industry sought employees to fill the factories in Piqua, Troy, Greenville. Bradford residents responded and many went to work in the Waco aircraft plant in near-by Troy.

By 1970 the railroad was no longer a contributor to the economy of the town. The great steam locomotives of the railroad were displaced in September of 1957. The coal station was closed and dynamited. The last tracks in the roundhouse were closed and the buildings abandoned. The shells of the abandoned buildings remain standing as a ghostly reminder of another era. The steam locomotive was replaced by the advances of technology and the diesel-electric locomotive. In 1985 the once busy tracks were abandoned by

Looking east at the intersection of Main Street and Miami Avenue, November, 1995. A Speedway Service station sits at the corner where Katherman's was in 1920. In the background is Iddings Park. The large brick house was built after the 1920 fire and replaced Dr. Bausman's former residence and office, destroyed in the fire. -- *Rev. Sandford Christophel photo*

a corporation that could hardly be called one ''in the public interest.''

No one used the railroad in town anyway. There have been three filling stations at the intersection of Main and Miami since the fire in 1920. The bank is still there and open for business. Patty's is right next door. The Masonic Lodge is right across the street where they were before the fire in 1920. Most of the boarding houses and hotels are gone, either having burned down, or fallen into disrepair and were demolished.

Today, the streets are all paved in town. They have been for many years. A factory sits on the right-of-way of the Second Division tracks to Gettysburg. A house obscures the view up the old Logansport Division right-of-way. The only reminders of the railroad include the ''Y'' Yard Park, the caboose and the railroad tower. Iddings Park, on the site of the fire is maintained, a quaint reminder of the man who once influenced the daily life of the town. His office and home is now the Bradford Public Library.

Looking east along the now abandoned roadbed of the Logansport Division of the Pennsylvania Railroad In 1920 three busy tracks crossed Miami Avenue here. About at the location of the white buildings in the background stood the Arnold and Iddings Elevator. At about the location of the white building in the left foreground was the Arnold Lumber Company office. The lumber yards were to the back, along the railroad. -- *Rev. Sandford Christophel photo*

The Bradford Volunteer Fire Department, once housed in a single bay of the village hall, today resides in a modern building in the ''Commons'' area of the railroad grounds. Their station building sits close to where the fire bell hung in 1920 at the time of the fire. The fire department consists of several pieces of modern fire fighting apparatus and an EMS service. The Pennsylvania Railroad Fire Bri-gade disappeared quietly in the 1920's. The only evidence of their existence are a few long-abandoned fire hydrants in the fields where the railroad shops once stood.

Looking around town, one finds the wounds healed from the railroad days. Street and sidewalk repair is evident, so is home remodeling and repair. The new generation who now reside in Bradford, are mostly

This 1995 view looks south toward the ''Y'' Yard. The photographer is standing in the area of the Arnold Lumber yard. The black foundation in the foreground of this view is that of the Arnold Lumber Company from the 1920 fire. Between the wall and the caboose is the abandoned right-of-way for the Logansport Division of the Pennsylvania Railroad. The Division post marker is sitting next to the caboose. It originally sat just west of Miami Avenue, where the Buckeye Division ended and the Logansport Division began. In earlier times train crews changed at the Division, thus the importance of Bradford to the Pennsylvania Railroad. The Division Post was moved to Union City, Indiana, in 1976, long after union regulations had abandoned the need to change crews at each Division. The caboose is part of a set of historical memorials to Bradford's heritage as a railroad town. It sits on the walkway to the Pennsylvania Railroad passenger station. The open area to its immediate right was the site for the massive Railway Y.M.C.A., demolished in the 1930's. The ''Y'' Yard Park was so named because it is the former property and site of the Railway Y.M.C.A. -- *Rev. Sandford Christophel photo*

Looking north on Miami Avenue, November, 1995. On the left is the Masonic Lodge building, which replaced a similar structure which burned in the 1920 fire. Other new buildings replaced structures destroyed in the fire. Behind the Speedway sign is the bank building, and to the right can be seen the top of Patty's IGA, where they relocated after the fire. *-- Rev. Sandford Christophel photo*

unaware of the town's past.

The famous Pumpkin Show remains the big attraction in town. It is the last vestige from the railroad era. Marching bands come from near and far for the fall event. It was started as a way to reinforce a sagging local economy back in the 1920's.

It is, for a younger generation, hard to imagine the hardship the residents of Bradford have endured -- and survived. But it is the American spirit to survive and prosper against all odds.

When it seems all is lost, there is always hope and determination. If you don't believe it, just look at the people in the village of Bradford.

Index

64